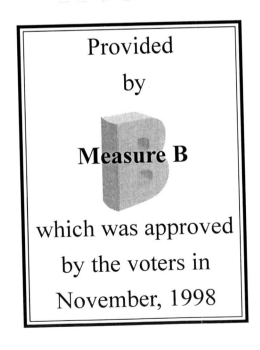

Provided

by

Measure B

which was approved

by the voters in

November, 1998

JAMES MONROE

ENCYCLOPEDIA
of PRESIDENTS

James Monroe

Fifth President of the United States

By Christine Maloney Fitz-Gerald

Consultant: Charles Abele, Ph.D.
Social Studies Instructor
Chicago Public School System

CHILDRENS PRESS ®

CHICAGO

Democratic-Republican Party campaign poster for the election of 1816, supporting James Monroe against Rufus King, the Federalist candidate. Monroe won.

Library of Congress Cataloging-in-Publication Data

Fitz-Gerald, Christine Maloney.
  James Monroe.

  (Encyclopedia of presidents)
  Includes index.
  Summary: The life and long political career of the
fifth president of the United States whose Monroe
Doctrine proclaimed opposition to further European
control in the Western hemisphere.
  1. Monroe, James, 1758-1831—Juvenile literature.
2. Presidents—United States—Biography—Juvenile
literature. [1. Monroe, James, 1758-1831.
2. Presidents] I. Title. II. Series.
E372.F57   1987   973.5′4′0924 [B] [92]   86-33436
ISBN 0-516-01383-1

Picture Acknowledgments

The Bettmann Archive—4, 5, 17, 18, 33, 37, 47
(2 photos), 48, 54 (2 photos), 58, 69, 70, 80, 81
(bottom), 86

Historical Pictures Service—9 (bottom), 10, 12,
13, 14, 25, 28, 30, 39, 40, 42, 44, 49, 52, 56, 63,
66, 74 (2 photos), 75 (2 photos), 81 (top left), 82
(right), 85 (top left and bottom), 89

Library of Congress—6, 22, 34, 51, 68, 82 (left)

National Archives—50, 78

Nawrocki Stock Photo—81 (top right)

North Wind Picture Archives—16, 19, 20, 24,
27

H. Armstrong Roberts—9 (top), 31, 35, 59, 64,
76, 85 (top right)

U.S. Bureau of Printing and Engraving—2

Cover design and illustration by
Steven Gaston Dobson

Childrens Press, Chicago
Copyright ©1987 by Regensteiner Publishing Enterprises, Inc.
All rights reserved. Published simultaneously in Canada.
Printed in the United States of America.

  13 14 15 16 17 18 19 20 R 02 01 00

James Monroe, fifth president of the United States

Table of Contents

Chapter 1

The Monroe Doctrine

The year was 1823. President James Monroe was sixty-five years old—eighteen years older than the United States of America. People knew him as a calm, patient man. But in 1823, he was alarmed.

Monroe had good reason to worry. It appeared that some European nations were ready to send armies to the Americas—not to any of the twenty-four states, but to South America. Several Spanish colonies in South America had recently won their freedom from Spain. They had set up governments much like the United States—with representatives and a constitution. But Russia, Prussia, Austria, and France were against this new form of government. They felt that every country should be ruled by a king.

Together these countries had massive armies. If they came over to crush the new free countries of South America, would they then attack the United States? Would they grab unsettled land in the West? The president had to decide what to do.

James Monroe had very much wanted to be president. He had a great desire to serve his country. Everyone admired his honesty. However, his ideas were not brilliant. He was so careful that he rarely made a quick political decision.

Monroe seemed very old-fashioned in 1823. Most men at this time wore trousers. Not the president. He still wore velvet knee breeches and silk stockings. Silver buckles shone on his shoes. His hair was powdered and tied back in the old-fashioned style. Atop his head was a three-cornered hat. Monroe was handsome, with striking blue-grey eyes, and stood almost six feet tall. But he dressed as men had dressed twenty years earlier.

The new country was changing fast. Steamboats were a frequent sight on the Mississippi River. Ships regularly sailed the thirty-day trip across the Atlantic Ocean. After six years' work, the Erie Canal would open soon. At first, people had laughed at the idea of a 340-mile-long canal, but now it seemed that it would work.

The tin can had just been introduced. Horse racing was the rage. Football was beginning to be played on college campuses. And the first American college for women, Troy Female Seminary, had just opened in New York State.

With all these changes going on around him, James Monroe still looked as if he lived in the past. That was because, once his mind was made up, he was stubborn. If he believed in something, he stuck by it.

As a young congressman, Monroe had been interested in the American West. He spoke for the rights of westerners and felt that the U.S. must add western states.

Above: The Erie Canal at Lockport, New York
Below: The steamship *Savannah*

Monroe explaining the Monroe Doctrine to his cabinet members

Even in 1823, some Americans thought that the West should be a different nation. They couldn't imagine one nation so large that it stretched from the Atlantic Ocean to the Pacific. Besides, Spain, Russia, and Great Britain all claimed chunks of western land. Even so, Monroe pictured all this land belonging to the United States someday.

James Monroe thought about the problems facing South American countries. He believed in their right to be free. He asked the advice of his friends Thomas Jefferson and James Madison. Finally his decision was made.

On December 2, 1823, Monroe went to the Capitol to speak before Congress. First, he announced that the U.S. would not allow foreign countries to send armies to any country in the Western Hemisphere (North and South America). The U.S. would be willing to go to war over this. Second, he said that no foreign nation could claim any more land in the Western Hemisphere. In return, Monroe told Congress, the U.S. would stay out of European wars.

Americans liked Monroe's speech, but they were not surprised by his words. It seemed perfectly clear to them that European powers had no right to meddle in the Americas. Why bother to make a speech about it?

The European nations, on the other hand, bitterly disliked being told what to do. They looked down on the U.S. as a small, second-rate power with no standing army, few citizens, and not much money. They chose to make no reply to Monroe's speech.

No one invaded South America, as it turned out. The Western Hemisphere was left in peace. This probably had more to do with a similar threat from England than with Monroe's warning. Nevertheless, later U.S. presidents—such as James Polk, Grover Cleveland, and Theodore Roosevelt—used Monroe's policy in facing foreign threats.

James Monroe's stand had been both brave and wise. It was brave because he had stood up to much more powerful nations at a time when the U.S. was not ready for war. But his speech was not a bluff—the U.S. would have been willing to fight. His stand was wise because he understood that the country must be willing to protect the freedom of the entire Western Hemisphere. He also preserved the American West for Americans.

The ideas in Monroe's speech came to be known as the Monroe Doctrine. The doctrine served the nation well for almost a hundred years. It was not until 1917 that the U.S. would fight in a European war, when it took part in World War I. This long period gave the country time to grow, to settle the West, and to become a first-rate power as James Monroe had hoped it would.

1. 1 Dec - 18th ia

Fellow Citizens of the Senate and
House of Representatives.

Many important subjects will claim
your attention during the present session,
of which I shall endeavour to give, in aid
of your deliberations, a just idea in this
communication. I undertake this duty
with diffidence, from the vast extent of
the interest, on which I have to treat, and
of their great importance to every portion
of our Union. I enter on it with zeal, from
a thorough conviction, that there never was
a period since the Establishment of our Revolution, when, regarding the condition
of the Civilized World, and its bearing on us,
there was greater necessity for devotion, in the
public servants to their respective duties,
or for virtue, patriotism, and union in our
Constituents.

Meeting in you a new Congress, I deem
it proper to present this view of public af-
fairs, in greater detail, than might other-
wise be necessary. I do it however with
peculiar satisfaction, from a knowledge
that in this respect, I shall comply more fully
with the sound principles of our Government.
The people being with us, exclusively the Sove-
reign, it is indispensable, that full informa-
tion be laid before them, on all important subjects, to enable them to exercise that high
power

The first page of the Monroe Doctrine

ment, confiding in its own strength, has less to apprehend from the other, and, in consequence each enjoying a greater freedom of action, is rendered more efficient for all the purposes for which it was instituted. It is unnecessary to treat here, of the vast improvement made in the system itself, by the adoption of this Constitution, and of its happy effect in elevating the character, and in protecting the rights of the Nation, as well as individuals. To what then do we owe these blessings? It is known to all, that we derive them from the excellence of our Institutions. Ought we not then ~~by these~~ to adopt every measure which may be necessary to perpetuate them?

Washington 2nd December
1823

James Monroe

The last page of the Monroe Doctrine, with Monroe's signature

James Monroe's birthplace in Westmoreland County, Virginia

Chapter 2

Growing Up in Virginia

James Monroe was a Virginian, born in Westmoreland County on April 28, 1758. In his lifetime, he would count three other famous Virginians as good friends—Thomas Jefferson, James Madison, and John Marshall, the fourth chief justice of the U.S. Supreme Court. Monroe also knew George Washington, another Virginian, but the two men were never close. Their age difference may have been a factor. Washington was a full twenty-six years older than James Monroe.

The Monroes were a solidly middle-class family. Spence Monroe, James's father, was a farmer and carpenter. The Monroes owned their own land, as did most colonists. They also owned slaves, as did many Virginians. The chief crop grown in Virginia was tobacco. Growing tobacco was hard on the soil, but the colonists grew it, year after year, because the British eagerly bought the whole crop. It seemed that a great many people in Britain chewed, smoked, or sniffed tobacco.

Virginians dancing the Virginia reel

Most of the colonists farmed, but only a few were carpenters. Carpenters were well respected and were in great demand. Because there were few architects in the thirteen colonies, carpenters both designed and built buildings. Often they copied building designs from books.

Like all sons of Virginia planters, James learned to ride well and to hunt game. He became an excellent horseman and a good shot with a rifle while he was still a boy. He was also lucky enough to go to school, something that very few colonial children had a chance to do. At school, his favorite subjects were Latin and mathematics.

Life in Virginia was merrier than life in the New England colonies. The Virginians attended church, but they also enjoyed dancing, singing, card playing and horse racing. Homes were built of either wood or brick, and none of them were comfortable by today's standards. Fireplaces provided the only heat. Since the houses were drafty, people rarely bathed. Toothbrushes were unknown.

Supplies from a British supply ship arrive in colonial Virginia.

The wonderful thing about life in the colonies, though, was that almost anyone could own land there. Almost any colonist could become richer by working hard. People ate well because the forests were filled with deer, rabbits, and squirrels. The streams and rivers teemed with fish.

Everything that people really needed, they could find in the colonies. But life's little luxuries — such as salt, sugar, and spices — came from abroad. If a family wanted fine furniture, paint, mirrors, clocks, or musical instruments, they had them shipped from Britain or France.

Americans preferred European clothes, as well. They followed European fashion as closely as they could. Everyday clothes were made in the colonies out of homespun cloth, but a family's Sunday-best clothing often came from abroad. Ships' captains who were sailing to Britain left with long lists of clothing materials that friends had asked them to buy. Of course, the materials they brought were often the wrong texture or color.

The iron foundry in Salisbury, Connecticut

At the time James Monroe was born, the colonies were engaged in the French and Indian War. This war was just a small echo of the massive fighting in Europe. Britain was completely absorbed in the Seven Years' War, so the colonies were left on their own. Slowly, they began to do more things for themselves. Soon after Monroe's birth, Americans were building four hundred ships a year, all for peaceful trade. Other American industries were beginning, as well. In 1762, Ethan Allen began an ironworks in Salisbury, Connecticut. Soon it would be producing cannons for the American Revolution.

The Treaty of Paris ended the Seven Years' War in 1763. Britain had won, but was left with huge debts. To support troops in the colonies, the British raised new taxes on newspapers, legal papers, glass, lead, paper, and tea. In protest, the Americans angrily boycotted, or refused to buy, these things.

The Boston Tea Party

In 1773, a group of colonists, dressed as Mohawk Indians, dumped over four hundred cases of British tea into Boston Harbor. This became known as the Boston Tea Party. The British were enraged. They closed Boston Harbor until the cost of the ruined tea was paid.

Northern colonists were furious with Britain because of new taxes on trade. Southern colonists were furious because the price of tobacco had dropped so sharply. Many Southerners were deeply in debt. They got very little for their crops, but had to pay high prices for goods they bought from Britain. It was in this tense political climate that James Monroe was heading off to college.

Chapter 3

The Soldier

In 1774, when he was sixteen years old, James Monroe rode to Williamsburg to attend William and Mary College. Williamsburg was the capital of Virginia and the biggest town that Monroe had ever seen. It had two hundred houses, and most were built of brick. The college had about a hundred students. But Monroe's stay at college was cut short by war.

On April 19, 1775, eight Americans were shot and killed by British soldiers in Lexington, Massachusetts. These American "minutemen" had died trying to stop the British redcoats from seizing a supply of muskets and other military supplies. No one knows which side fired first. But this was the battle that began the American Revolution.

News of the Battle of Lexington reached William and Mary College nine days later, on Monroe's seventeenth birthday. The students formed militias at once, and Monroe joined a company. He was part of a small group of students who broke into the royal governor's palace in Norfolk to find muskets.

Opposite page: William and Mary College

George Washington crossing the Delaware River

James Monroe never lacked bravery or physical energy. He was aching to join the fight. Traveling north with a company of other young men, he joined General George Washington's army in New York. He saw his first battles in the fall of 1776, at Harlem Heights (now Central Park) and at White Plains. The Americans managed to push the British back but, badly outnumbered, they began a retreat. Throughout November, they retreated across New Jersey. Monroe and his company rode ahead as scouts, alert for any sign of British troops.

In December 1776, the army crossed the Delaware River into Pennsylvania. They felt safe for the moment, but their spirits were low. They needed a victory.

At this point, it didn't seem that such a small group of men could really win the war. They were a very unusual-looking army. The soldiers dressed in various outfits, many of them wearing fringed hunting shirts. As frontier riflemen, they were good shots, but they were generally poor at following orders. They had no idea how to form up for a battle. Every man did exactly as he pleased.

Many colonists refused to support this tiny army. It was not that they were loyal to Britain; they were simply neutral. Many Americans were content to wait and see who would win. General Washington wanted a big victory to persuade neutral Americans to support the revolutionary army. More importantly, he hoped for a victory that would persuade some of his soldiers to reenlist. For many of the men, their term of service was finished on New Year's Day. Without a win, many would simply go home.

On Christmas Day, the revolutionary army crossed the Delaware once again into New Jersey. The crossing was dangerous, since the river was filled with huge chunks of ice. It was snowing and there was a strong wind. The trips back and forth seemed endless; not only did men have to be moved, but horses and cannon as well.

The American plan was to attack Trenton, New Jersey. There Hessian mercenaries (German soldiers-for-hire) were celebrating Christmas with drinking, eating, singing, and games. A local Tory (a pro-British American) wrote a note to warn the Hessians that the Americans were coming. But the Hessian commander, Colonel Johann Rall, never read the note. He was too busy playing cards. He stuffed the unread note into his pocket.

The surprise attack at Trenton

In the snowy night, James Monroe stood guard at a crossroad as the boats crossed and recrossed the river. A farmer came up to Monroe and his men and told them to get off his land. James Monroe refused. When the farmer realized that these men were Americans, not Hessians, he brought them food and drink. When the entire army was finally assembled, the farmer told Monroe that he was coming with them to Trenton. He was a doctor and felt he could help the wounded.

On the six-mile trek to Trenton, the men marched along in the dark night as quietly as they could. One soldier remembered that the torches attached to the cannon "sparkled and blazed in the storm." When the army reached Trenton, it was already dawn. Even so, the Hessians were completely surprised. The mercenaries fired

Colonel Rall surrenders to George Washington after the Battle of Trenton

wildly from windows. Then they ran into the streets. Some were trying to turn the cannon around in the narrow street so they could fire on the Americans. Lieutenant James Monroe and Captain William Washington led an attack on them. An American soldier wrote that they "took two pieces [cannon] in the act of firing." It was a brave act. But James Monroe received a serious bullet wound in the shoulder. If the doctor he had met during the night had not been there, he would have died.

For the Americans, it was a stunning victory. They captured a thousand Hessian soldiers, many guns, and fifteen regimental flags. For his bravery, James Monroe was promoted to captain. He was ferried across the river to recover from his wounds in a local home.

By the summer of 1777, Monroe was well enough to rejoin the army. He was made an aide to General William Alexander, known as Lord Stirling. After the Battle of Brandywine in September 1777, he was made a major.

The following winter was a dismal one. While the British rested comfortably in Philadelphia, the Americans starved at Valley Forge. The winter was so hard that some 2,500 soldiers died of cold and hunger.

Monroe spent the winter with Stirling in Reading, Pennsylvania. The officers there had better food and shelter than the other soldiers. But they too ate little.

Great news came in the spring; France had become an ally of the United States. When Washington told his troops, "there were a thousand hats tossed in the air."

In June, the army left Valley Forge. On the eve of the Battle of Monmouth, he acted as scout. He captured three British soldiers and sent a short note to General Washington to tell him where the British were camped.

The Battle of Monmouth was fought on a scorching hot day. It was then that a woman named Mary Ludwig Hayes won a place in history as "Molly Pitcher." Ignoring the flying bullets, she carried water to the wounded.

By now, Monroe wanted to lead men himself. He rode off to Virginia with a letter from Washington. Washington had written that Monroe was "a brave, active, and sensible officer" who deserved to command soldiers. Despite such high praise, Monroe could not find enough soldiers to lead. He had to wait.

The time was not wasted. He studied law and became an aide to Thomas Jefferson, the brilliant governor of

Molly Pitcher at the Battle of Monmouth

Virginia. The two would come to be great friends. Finally, in the summer of 1780, Monroe got his soldiers. The British attacked Virginia, and Virginians rushed to sign up for military duty. James became colonel of an entire regiment. He fought to the end of the war.

The end came in 1781, with the British defeat at Yorktown. The British military band played a tune called "The World Turned Upside Down," and so it seemed to them. The Virginians celebrated the peace at a festive dance held at a local Fredericksburg tavern. George Washington was there. So was James Monroe. A veteran of many battles at the age of twenty-three, he had proved his bravery and competence time and again. What would peacetime bring?

Second Street in Philadelphia in the 1700s. Monroe served as U.S. senator here when Philadelphia was the capital of the country.

Chapter 4

Diplomacy

Many soldiers find it hard to return to everyday life after a war. James Monroe was no exception. Anxious and restless after the war, he didn't know what to do next.

His father, Spence Monroe, had been a farmer. But after his father died, James Monroe had sold the large family farm. An army career did not appeal to him. Americans did not even want a national army. Now that the war with Britain was over, the army melted away. Monroe had liked studying law, however, and he decided to continue his studies in France or England. But before he could leave the country, he was asked to serve in the Virginia General Assembly. A life of public service was beginning.

In 1782, at the age of twenty-four, Monroe was one of the youngest members of the assembly. It was a rowdy group. An observer wrote that the representatives would "talk of horses, run-away slaves, yesterday's play, politics." They seemed interested in everything except making laws. It was a strange-looking group, as well: "There are displayed boots, trousers, stockings and Indian leggings, great coats, and short jackets."

Delegates arriving at the Annapolis Convention in Maryland

Here James Monroe met another young man who was serious about the business of government—James Madison, who was leaving the assembly just as Monroe joined it. The two men liked each other instantly, and this marked the beginning of a long friendship.

In 1783, James Monroe was asked to represent Virginia at the Fourth Continental Congress. That fall, Congress met in Annapolis, Maryland. Monroe was pleased to find Thomas Jefferson there, and the two often ate together. The Fourth Congress needed to approve a peace treaty with Great Britain. The war in America had now been over for a year and a half. Clever Benjamin Franklin had gone to Paris to negotiate a peace with Britain. He had done a good job. But many states never sent representatives to the Fourth Congress, so the Congress didn't have enough members to approve a treaty for a very long time. The treaty would not be signed until January 1784.

A home in the western frontier

There were other important problems for the Fourth Congress to solve. Should new states be admitted to the U.S.? How should western land be divided into states? Thomas Jefferson was in favor of simply drawing the states on the map. He thought that all the new states should be roughly equal in size. James Monroe had a very different feeling. While Congress was in recess, he traveled to see the land for himself.

Monroe was a tireless traveler in an age when most people were happy simply to stay at home. Travel in the frontier was not only exhausting; it was also dangerous. Monroe wrote to Jefferson, "I will certainly see all that my time will admit of. It is possible I may lose my scalp from the temper of the Indians but if either a little fighting or a great deal of running will save it, I shall escape safe." In fact, three men in Monroe's group were killed by the Indians, but Monroe returned safely.

Monroe was impressed by the grandeur of the land. He persuaded Congress that drawing lines on a map simply would not do. The boundary lines for the new states were already there. Nature had drawn them. They were the mountains, the lakes, and the rivers. The new states would not be of equal size, but that was not important.

Monroe had not traveled as far as the Mississippi River. However, he understood how important that river was to the people on the frontier. They needed the Mississippi to get their crops to market. The Spanish claimed to own the Mississippi and wanted the U.S. to recognize their ownership. Eastern businessmen, having little to gain from the river, were perfectly willing to give up American claims to the Mississippi. In return, they hoped to receive a new trade treaty with Spain. But Monroe saw that this bargain would be unfair to the frontier people. "It will be for the benefit of the U.S. that the river should be opened," he said. He fought to prevent the U.S. from giving up its claim to the Mississippi. Once he was made the chairman of the Congress's Mississippi Committee, he was able to get what he wanted.

Although Monroe had won, he was discouraged by the selfishness of the states. No one seemed to care about the common good. Furthermore, he was broke. Congressmen's salaries were low, and the payments were often late. Monroe decided it was time to return to practicing law.

He chose Fredericksburg, Virginia, as a good place to start a law practice. When he moved there, he brought his new wife. She had been Elizabeth Kortright of New York City. Monroe had met her while Congress was meeting in

Elizabeth Kortright, James Monroe's wife

New York. Elizabeth was a tall and beautiful woman. Her family was wealthy and well known in New York society. Many New Yorkers were startled when she married James Monroe, an "unknown" congressman from the South.

For a while, life in Fredericksburg was everything Monroe wanted. He worked every day in a one-story brick building in the center of town. His marriage was happy. A daughter, Eliza, was born on July 27, 1787. In a letter to his friend Thomas Jefferson, Monroe wrote, "Mrs. Monroe hath added a daughter to our society, who tho noisy, adds greatly to its amusement."

Gradually, though, life as a small-town lawyer lost its charm. Life in Fredericksburg was not moving fast enough for James Monroe. He longed to be back in public office.

The Monroes' Ash Lawn estate

To his great disappointment, he was not asked to serve in the Constitutional Convention, though he was asked to be on the Virginia Ratifying Committee. But when Monroe read the Constitution that the convention members had written, he was disturbed. Nothing at all was said about the rights of the individual! When votes were taken, Monroe voted against accepting the Constitution. The Constitution was approved, but it was a close vote. Later a Bill of Rights was added. It spelled out the freedoms for which the Revolution had been fought.

In 1789, the Monroes moved to Charlottesville, Virginia, and built their home, Ash Lawn. Monroe wished to be near his good friend, Thomas Jefferson. Jefferson was in Paris but his home, Monticello, was right outside of Charlottesville.

The city of Philadelphia, seen from a riverside park

By 1790, Monroe was eager to return to government. He ran for the U.S. Senate and won. The thirty-two-year-old senator was off to Philadelphia, the temporary capital. The largest city in the U.S., with a population of 42,000, Philadelphia was a natural choice for the capital.

Senator Monroe soon realized that one of the biggest issues in the U.S. was, oddly enough, the French Revolution. Already, Americans were splitting into political parties over the French Revolution, which began in 1789. Some Americans strongly supported the French Revolution. At home, they were interested in the problems of farmers and of westerners. They were known as Republicans. Others, called Federalists, wanted to have stronger ties with Great Britain. In the U.S., they seemed to favor the interests of city dwellers and eastern businessmen.

Finally, in 1793, the French declared war on Great Britain. They had just executed their king on the guillotine. By this time, many Americans were horrified at the bloodiness of the French Revolution. Worse yet, the U.S. was still an ally of France, at least on paper. The French, who had come to the aid of the U.S. in the American Revolution, now fully expected some help in their own war. The U.S. had to choose a friend and make an enemy.

President George Washington sent Republican James Monroe to France as U.S. minister. Washington, however, had no intention of joining France in a war against Britain. As a Federalist, Washington wished the U.S. to draw closer to Great Britain. He appointed John Jay U.S. minister to Britain. Jay was to negotiate a treaty with the British that would resolve many disputes between the two countries.

No one told Monroe the full truth about the Jay Treaty, and so he assured the French that nothing big was afoot. When the news of the completed Jay Treaty reached the French, they were furious, though not with James Monroe. The French truly liked him. They were angry with the United States government. However, President Washington *was* angry with Monroe. He felt that Monroe had not kept a proper distance with the French. He had promised them too much and become too friendly. Monroe was recalled in disgrace.

Because a winter crossing of the Atlantic was far too dangerous, Monroe did not go home at once. Instead, he took his family on a tour of Europe. Although Washington sent a new minister to France to replace James Monroe, the French refused to accept another minister from the U.S.

Citizens angry about the Jay Treaty burn an effigy of John Jay.

Monroe was hurt. He was a straightforward man, and he had done what he felt was right. He had never disguised the fact that he was a Republican and, therefore, pro-French. Since Washington had appointed him to the position anyway, he had assumed that he was free to be himself. He had represented his own views rather than the views of Washington's Federalist government.

When the Monroes finally arrived home in the summer of 1797, Monroe's political future looked bleak. Washington was still angry. His successor, John Adams, was also a Federalist. He would have no use for James Monroe. Virginians, however, were delighted to have Monroe at home. They elected him governor in 1799. As governor of Virginia, Monroe improved the schools and the roads. Many new public buildings were built. The Potomac and James rivers were dredged to allow larger ships to navigate them. But tragedy struck the Monroes when their baby son died after a series of illnesses.

While Monroe governed Virginia, his political fortunes improved. His Republican party was on the rise, and the power of the Federalists was on the wane. In 1800, Thomas Jefferson was elected president. Then in 1803 he asked James Monroe to return to France to engage in some important negotiations. Spain had just ceded the Louisiana Territory to France, and the port of New Orleans was closed to American ships. Jefferson wanted Monroe to see if the U.S. could buy New Orleans from Napoleon Bonaparte, France's ambitious and ruthless emperor. Jefferson sent Monroe off, telling him that "the whole public hope will be rested on you."

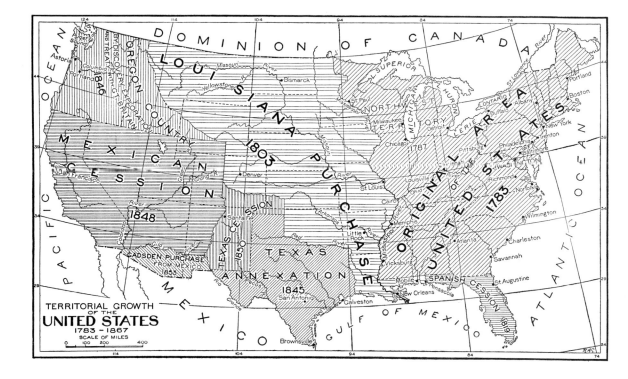

TERRITORIAL GROWTH OF THE UNITED STATES 1783-1867

The U.S. already had a minister in France, Robert Livingston. He had been trying to talk the French into selling New Orleans for some time, with no success. So he was amazed when Napoleon suddenly announced that he would sell not only New Orleans but the entire Louisiana Territory. Shortly after this astonishing change in policy, Monroe arrived in Paris. He felt very ill because the Atlantic crossing had been stormy. But he and Livingston went to work at once. They haggled over the price for a week. Then a figure was agreed upon—$15 million.

The American ministers were not quite sure what they were buying for their $15 million. The boundaries of the Louisiana Territory were fuzzy in everyone's minds. They asked the French minister, Talleyrand, for help, but he gave them a very offhand reply: "I can give you no direction. You have made a noble bargain for yourselves and I suppose you will make the most of it."

A "press gang" in New York, impressing men for the British navy

As it turned out, the U.S. had acquired a huge chunk of land—almost a million square miles. The eastern border was the Mississippi River. The western border ran along the Rocky Mountains. In the north, the territory touched the present-day Canadian border. In the south, it reached the Gulf of Mexico.

With Britain and France at war, the United States faced new dangers. British ships were stopping American ships, taking American sailors, and forcing them to serve in the British navy. This was called impressment. Jefferson sent Monroe to Britain to try to put a stop to this, but the British ignored Monroe's requests. They were also rude to him and his family. This may have been partly Thomas Jefferson's fault. The American president was a very casual man. On one occasion, for instance, he had worn bedroom slippers to a meeting with the British minister. The British found this sort of informality very offensive and they disliked Americans as it was.

Making no headway with the British, Monroe set off to Spain to discuss Florida. Spain had agreed to give Florida to France in 1800, so the U.S. had thought that the Louisiana Purchase would include Florida. Now it was 1805 and Spain still held it. Jefferson wanted Monroe to try to buy it.

After a mule trip over the Pyrenees Mountains, Monroe arrived in Madrid. But the Spanish refused to even talk about Florida. Monroe returned to London, only to find that things had gotten much worse. The British had passed a law that allowed them to capture any American ship that was carrying war goods to France. That meant that every American merchant ship had to stop in England to be searched. The French, in turn, said that they would seize any ship that obeyed this British rule. American trade with Europe was ruined. Monroe thought that he could do no more, and so he sailed for home.

Diplomacy had been very trying for James Monroe. His first mission to France in 1796 had ended when he was recalled in disgrace. He had helped to bring about the Louisiana Purchase in 1803. But from 1803 to 1807, he had been ignored and insulted in London and Madrid. He had not been able to buy Florida for the U.S. He had not stopped British impressment of American sailors. He had also come to distrust the French under Napoleon. "We have no sincere friends anywhere," he wrote.

At home, Virginians welcomed him again. For a second time, they elected him governor of Virginia. His friend James Madison succeeded Jefferson as president. Madison would soon turn to Monroe for help.

The British burn Washington, D.C., during the War of 1812.

Chapter 5

At War Again

When James Madison became president, Monroe felt certain that he himself would be secretary of state. He couldn't hide his disappointment when Madison chose Robert Smith instead. But Madison fired Smith in 1811. Then he asked Monroe to take the job.

It wasn't an easy task. The secretary of state dealt with foreign countries. France and Britain were at war, and Napoleon was determined to ruin Great Britain. Neither Britain nor France would honor U.S. neutrality. Neither wished the U.S. to trade with the other. American ships were being harassed. American crewmen were being taken prisoner. And American ships and their cargoes were being confiscated or burned.

Americans were most angry about the British policy of impressing American sailors into service on British warships. The British claimed that the men they took were deserters from the Royal Navy. Some were. Many British sailors jumped at the chance to desert and to serve on an American ship. Life in the Royal Navy was unbelievably horrible. A British seaman faced a life of brutal discipline, rotten food, filthy living quarters, and poor pay. Life aboard American ships was heaven by comparison.

British officers impressing American sailors into service

Nevertheless, most impressed American sailors were not deserters. But the British did not care. They needed sailors to fight in the war against Napoleon. British warships were always undermanned, and many of their sailors were dying in the endless war with France.

Monroe had gone round and round with the British on the subject of impressment. He had years of experience in walking the narrow line between France and England. Formerly, he had favored the French. Now, because he distrusted Napoleon, he tended to favor the British. But he was not enthusiastic about either country. It was a matter of choosing the lesser of two evils. As Jefferson put it, "As for France and England, the one is a den of robbers, the other of pirates."

Although Monroe was partial to the British, he made no progress with them. Soon, British men-of-war were hovering right outside New York Harbor. They swooped down on American ships as soon as they cleared the harbor. This was too much for Americans to bear. On June 18, 1812, Congress declared war on Great Britain.

The War of 1812 should never have happened. Two days before the U.S. declared war, Britain announced that it would stop impressing American sailors. The war could have been called off, except for one thing—during the several weeks that it took for the news to reach America, American armies invaded Canada but were badly beaten. Now Americans felt that they could not quit the war without a victory. Even Monroe felt this way. He wrote that if the British asked for peace, he would say, "No, I will not treat with you now. Wait till we have given you a better opinion of us." Americans would soon wish that they had ended this war while they had a chance.

The British had been stunned by the U.S. declaration of war. They had no wish to fight another costly war. Nevertheless, they began to fight. By 1814, the land war was going very badly for the U.S.

James Monroe was longing to leave his desk job and take a military command. He dreamed of raising an army to recapture the city of Detroit, now in British hands. It was difficult for a man of his energy to sit in Washington while the war was going so badly. It now looked as though the war was coming to Washington, D.C. In 1814, the British landed an army on the coast of Maryland's Chesapeake Bay. They began marching toward Washington.

General Armstrong, the secretary of war, told President Madison not to worry. The British, he said, would not attack Washington. Armstrong believed that they would attack Baltimore, Maryland, instead. So no trenches were dug to protect Washington. General Winder, who was in charge of defending the city, made no battle plans. On August 18, Monroe told Madison that the British certainly were coming to Washington. He advised Madison to begin to remove important government files. Then Monroe set out on horseback to scout the British advance.

Monroe found some local militia gathered in the town of Bladensburg and tried to rearrange them into a battle line. Finally General Winder arrived. The American troops were so disorganized and so poorly led that they melted away in front the British fire. A British admiral commented that the "American army seemed to be made of cheese."

People were fleeing Washington with all they could carry. President Madison and his wife, Dolley, were with them. The Madisons, Monroe, and other government officials fled to Virginia to avoid capture. On August 24, the British walked into Washington almost without firing a shot. When they entered the White House, they found the table set for lunch. They sat down and ate the meal that Dolley had prepared for President Madison. Afterwards, they made a large pile of the White House furniture and set the White House ablaze. They also burned the Capitol, Navy Yard, and the bridge across the Potomac. A wild rainstorm on August 25 put out the fires. The British slipped away to their ships and sailed to Baltimore.

Right: Dolley Madison saves
the Declaration of Independence
as she flees the White House.

Below: The Capitol
Building after the fire

Francis Scott Key finds that the star-spangled banner still waves.

Luckily, Baltimore had much tougher defenses. The British bombarded Fort McHenry, which protected the city, but Fort McHenry would not surrender. Francis Scott Key was an American prisoner on a British ship during the bombardment. Seeing the American flag still flying above the fort after a night of fighting, he wrote "The Star-Spangled Banner." This song became the national anthem.

President Madison returned to Washington in a rage. He fired Secretary of War Armstrong. Then he asked Monroe, whom he trusted, to be the new secretary. He also asked him to be military commander in the District of Columbia. James Monroe was now secretary of state, secretary of war,

The bullet-ridden flag that flew over Fort McHenry

and a military commander. He needed every bit of his immense physical energy now. For an entire month, he barely slept. As secretary of state, he now wished to talk to Britain about a peace.

But the British were in no rush to end the war. They had just defeated Napoleon, who had foolishly invaded Russia in June of 1812. When the harsh Russian winter set in, he had been forced to retreat. He had lost most of his army to the Russians and to cold and hunger. Although he tried to raise a new army, his power was broken. He was forced to give up being the emperor of France in April of 1814. With their old enemy destroyed, the British were free to settle old scores with their former colonies.

The USS *Constitution,* nicknamed "Old Ironsides"

Americans had little to cheer about so far in the land war, but they had some dazzling victories at sea. American sailors were much better paid and better treated than British sailors. While British ships were low on manpower, some American ships, such as "Old Ironsides," had crews who were all volunteers. Commodore Oliver Hazard Perry defeated an entire squadron of British ships on Lake Erie with a much smaller fleet. After the battle, he sent his famous message, "We have met the enemy and they are ours."

The war dragged on. As secretary of state, James Monroe pursued peace talks with the British. But as secretary of war, he kept on directing the war effort. Negotiators from both countries met in Europe to talk peace.

Jackson at the Battle of New Orleans

Finally, on Christmas Eve, 1814, the Treaty of Ghent was signed. This simply restored to each country all the land it had owned before. Nothing was said about the freedom of the seas—the issue that had started the war.

Before news of the signed peace treaty reached the United States, there was one last battle, it seemed a fitting end to the the War of 1812. War had been declared after the reason to fight was gone. Now the Americans would have their land victory—but after a peace treaty had been signed. By now, the war had put the U.S. into financial trouble. The country was actually bankrupt. Somehow, Monroe raised enough money to buy guns and supplies for an army headed by General Andrew Jackson. Marching head-on into Jackson's strong defenses, the British lost hundreds of men. The Americans lost barely a handful. Jackson became famous as "The Hero of New Orleans." Monroe was simply thankful that the war was over.

A scene in front of the Philadelphia State House at the time of the 1816 election

Chapter 6

The Presidency—
Setting the Stage

It was clear to everyone that James Monroe would be the next president. Certainly, the American people liked him. They admired the way he had conducted himself during the War of 1812. This war had not held many bright spots for the U.S., but Monroe had been a positive force. He had been active and decisive.

When Monroe ran for president in 1816, he won in most states. Only Massachusetts, Connecticut, and Delaware did not support him. Monroe took office as fifth president of the United States in 1817, with Daniel Tompkins of New York as his vice-president.

Every president chooses men to fill the jobs in his cabinet. These are the men who will help him to run the country during his term. The most important cabinet job is secretary of state. James Monroe had a talent for friendship. He always surrounded himself with very bright and capable men.

Left: John Quincy Adams.   Right: Henry Clay

Monroe knew there were people who felt that Virginians had too much power in the national government. Of the first five presidents, four had been Virginians. George Washington, Thomas Jefferson, James Madison, and, now, James Monroe. Only the second president, John Adams of Massachusetts, had been from another state. Monroe wished the entire country to feel a part of the national government. He resolved to pick a northerner as his secretary of state. He appointed John Quincy Adams, the son of ex-president John Adams.

This choice pleased many people. It also made an enemy for Monroe. Henry Clay, a southerner and the Speaker of the House of Representatives, had wished to be secretary of state. Clay was so bitter that he tried to ruin Monroe's inauguration ceremony. On inauguration day, the president-elect took the oath of office. Up until now, this ceremony had always been held indoors, in the Capitol building. But Henry Clay, as Speaker of the House, refused to let Monroe take the oath indoors. Clay argued that the floor of the building might break because of the weight of the crowd. Luckily, the day of the ceremony was sunny and mild. The affair was such a success that, ever since, presidents have taken the oath of office outdoors.

Monroe had a clear idea of what he wished to do as president. He had traveled a great deal and he knew that the country needed more roads and canals. He was also concerned with American military strength. With the exception of its navy, the U.S. had fought very poorly in the War of 1812. Monroe had no desire to go to war again. But he did want the U.S. to have a well-trained standing army. The forts along the east coast needed to be repaired. "We must support our rights or lose our character," he said. If the U.S. were more prepared for war, this might actually help to prevent war. Other countries would hesitate to bother American ships and American citizens.

Before working on these problems, Monroe went on a three-month tour of the country. It puzzled some people. They felt that it was a frivolous waste of time. They failed to see what Monroe was doing. But he understood that a president must have the support of the entire country if he wants to get a lot done. The War of 1812 had divided the country. New England had been so opposed to the war that the New England states had thought about leaving the U.S. Monroe wished to heal any remaining bitterness.

Monroe on his tour of the country

Monroe's tour took him as far north as Portland, Maine, and as far west as Detroit. He would tour the South later, in 1819. He traveled by horse, by carriage, by steamboat, and, at times, afoot.

The tour turned into a triumphal procession. Americans loved James Monroe. Large crowds lined the streets as he passed through towns and cities. There were bands, parades, gun salutes, and parties. In New England, the president was showered with flower petals. Newspapers wrote of Monroe in glowing terms. One newspaper called the times "The Era of Good Feeling," and the phrase stuck. Monroe's terms as president would be known as "The Era of Good Feeling." For at least the first term, this was true. Americans did feel good about their country.

What did Americans think of their new president? They were impressed by his plain and straightforward manner. He was a tall man. The expression on his face was usually serious. His blue-grey eyes were his best feature. When he smiled, he became handsome.

It was a bit odd that Monroe dressed in the old style. Younger men were now wearing trousers rather than knee breeches. Men had given up their wigs and women had given up their whalebone corsets. Fashionable men no longer wore their hair long and tied back with a ribbon. They cut it short. But Monroe's old-fashioned appearance endeared him to Americans. It reminded them of the American Revolution.

If the country was impressed with the new president, the new president was equally impressed with the country. In early 1817, there were nineteen states. Most people still farmed for a living, but new industries were growing. Philadelphia, the largest city, was also the most sophisticated city. It was filled with neat brick buildings on tree-lined streets. The streets were paved and there was a city water system. (Washington, D.C., still had pigs and cows grazing on the grass that grew in the streets.) Philadelphia was also the center of science and art in the U.S. Monroe visited the Philadelphia Academy of Fine Arts, a famous medical school, and a marvelous natural history museum. This museum was started by a painter named Charles Wilson Peale. It boasted a variety of stuffed birds and beasts, but it was most famous for its display of a complete mastodon skeleton. Peale himself had helped to excavate the prehistoric skeleton.

Robert Fulton's steamboat, the *Clermont*

During his tour, Monroe also became impressed with the steamboat. Robert Fulton had built the first steamboat, the *Clermont*, in 1807. The *Clermont* could travel five miles per hour. That may not sound very fast, but the importance of the steamboat did not lie in its speed.

Before the steamboat, most river transportation moved downstream. Getting a boat to go upstream was back-breaking work. Men on the boat used long poles to push the boat forward. Mules on the shore towed the boat upstream with ropes attached to their harnesses. This was so difficult that few boats were taken upstream. Typically, a boat would be built for a trip downriver. When the journey was over, the boat was broken apart and the wood was sold. The crew would travel home on foot.

A pioneer family beginning a new life in the frontier

Monroe saw that Americans were moving west in a steady stream. Out west, land was cheap. New England farmers, tired of rocky soil and harsh winters, moved west. Southern farmers, when they could no longer grow enough crops on the tired soil of the old South, moved west. New immigrants, mostly Irish and German, moved west as well.

The West seemed to offer wealth and independence, but life there was hard. Forests stretched from the Appalachian Mountains to the Mississippi. Homesteaders had to clear the woods with axes. Often they simply burned a clearing in the woods. Some European visitors wrote that the people who lived on the American frontier were terribly pale from living constantly in the shade of the vast forests. On the frontier, food was plain and clothing was rough. Doctors were scarce. Once in a while, a traveling minister came by. Worst of all was the terrible loneliness. But the frontier people made work an occasion for fun. They held barn raisings and cornhuskings.

Frontier life, as hard as it was, suited some people. They moved west again and again. They would clear a patch of land and farm it for a while. When more settlers moved in around them, the original settlers—feeling crowded— would sell their land and move on.

Monroe was, as always, fascinated by the West. Of the five new states admitted to the U.S. during his two terms as president—Mississippi, Illinois, Alabama, Maine, and Missouri—four were in the West.

By September of 1817, James Monroe was back in Washington. The Monroes moved into the White House soon after his return. While he had been touring the country, workmen had been repairing the White House, badly damaged during the War of 1812. The walls were painted white to hide the ugly burn marks. All of Washington was waiting for the Monroes to entertain. Dolley Madison, the last White House hostess, had been an especially charming and energetic woman. While James Madison was president, the White House was known for its festive dinners and parties. Businessmen, senators, and foreign diplomats could drop in to see the president at any time. Dolley visited the wives of new diplomats as soon as they arrived in Washington. Everyone was sure that the Monroes would want to entertain in the same way.

They were mistaken. Elizabeth Monroe soon let Washington know that she would not be visiting the wives of all the new diplomats and congressmen. James Monroe would not see people who just appeared at the door of the White House. From now on, everyone had to make an appointment to see the president. Washington was in an uproar over these changes. The social life of the city revolved around the White House. No one liked the new rules.

The Monroes had a reason for these changes. Both of the Monroes understood that Europeans were often offended at American manners. Americans were open and informal. The Monroes had spent many years living in France and England. In these countries, people respected ceremony and formality. James Monroe well remembered how he and his family had been snubbed by English society. The British had treated them rudely because they thought President Jefferson was rude to British diplomats. The British minister always wore his fanciest clothes and all of his medals when he called upon President Jefferson. But Jefferson was known to wear his bedroom slippers and a shirt that needed to be cleaned. Jefferson had meant no harm. He was simply a very casual person. But the English minister had been very angry.

Americans loved Monroe for his simple, honest manner. But as president, he became more formal. He thought it would be easier to work wih foreign diplomats if the White House were a less casual place. Even the White House furniture was different. Much of the furniture had been burned by the British during the War of 1812. New furniture was badly needed. So the Monroes sold the government some of their own furniture to be used in the White House. Most of it had been bought in France during the French Revolution and was quite ornate. In all, the government paid the Monroes over $9,000 for White House furniture, dishes, and silver. The Monroes actually sold it for less than it was worth. Later, James Monroe would regret this sale. Congress would accuse him of charging too much money for his furniture. Eventually, Monroe bought his furniture back.

Elizabeth Monroe was not in good health. She could not have entertained as much as Dolley Madison had. Every year, there were more congressmen and more diplomats. Washington and the country were growing wildly. The Monroes had two daughters, Eliza and Maria. The older of the two, Eliza, was asked to help in entertaining. Eliza was twenty-nine when her father became president. She did help her parents with parties and dinners, but she was very haughty.

On the other hand, everyone found the younger daughter, Maria, very appealing. But she was much too young to help with social duties. Maria was only fourteen years old in 1817. At the age of sixteen, she married Samuel Gouverneur, her father's personal secretary.

Maria Monroe Gouverneur, James Monroe's daughter

For a long time, Washington society boycotted the Monroes' parties. No one would attend Mrs. Monroe's open houses. But the Monroes stuck by their new rules. Slowly, people began to attend White House teas and parties again, but they were not as much fun as they had been in Dolley Madison's day. One congressman said of a White House party that "everyone looked as if the next moment would be his last."

But while Washingtonians complained, European visitors actually felt more at ease in the White House. They understood formality—it was familiar to them. Elizabeth Monroe actually made things easier for future First Ladies. Never again would a First Lady be expected to entertain as much as Dolley Madison had. No longer would people expect a First Lady to visit the wife of every congressman and diplomat. The Monroes had begun a new order of things in the capital. Now the stage was set.

Chapter 7

The First Term

Two large issues arose during James Monroe's first term. The first problem was a familiar one: Spain still owned Florida, and the U.S. still wanted to buy it. With a lot of hard work and patience, Monroe would solve the Florida problem. But the second problem was far worse. North and South were beginning to split apart over slavery. This problem would not be solved. It would only be put off for forty years, until the Civil War.

Florida had been a thorn in the side of the U.S. for a long time. The U.S. government had hoped that the Louisiana Purchase of 1803 was meant to include Florida. It did not. In 1804, Monroe had spent five months in Madrid trying to buy Florida for the U.S. Spain would not sell. Now, in 1818, the U.S. wanted Florida even more. It was not that Americans considered it to be such a beautiful, rich, or desirable land. They wanted Florida because it was the home of violent outlaws who raided Georgia to steal cattle. Many people were killed in these raids. Always the bandits would escape back into Florida, out of the reach of the law. They were safe on Spanish land. Many black slaves ran away to Florida, too. And Indians who had been driven from their own lands into Florida also led raids.

Jackson's troops charging into Pensacola, Florida

The violence along the Florida border became so bad that, in 1818, President Monroe decided to send General Andrew Jackson into Florida to restore order. Jackson believed that he had authority to do whatever it took to defeat the Indians—even to attack the Spanish. Monroe later denied that he had granted Jackson that much power.

Andrew Jackson was certainly not the best choice for a mission like this. He was brave and decisive, but he had a bad temper. He was reckless. And he was certain that he was always right about everything. Monroe should have realized that Jackson was the wrong man for the job when the general offered to capture all of Florida. "It will be done in six days," said Jackson. So when he marched his several thousand men into Florida, he immediately captured the Spanish fort of Saint Mark's. There he killed two British captives, one a trader and the other a soldier. Then Jackson marched on the Spanish town of Pensacola, which he captured.

Jackson had gone too far, far beyond his orders. He had taken Spanish towns and forts by force, and he had killed two British men. Monroe was shocked. Now both Spain and England were furious. Secretary of State John Quincy Adams was trying to persuade the Spanish to sell Florida when the bad news arrived. The timing could not have been worse.

Monroe called an emergency meeting of his cabinet. He was in a tight spot, yet he did not show his anger. He was calm and good-natured. While he was quite angry with Jackson, he also understood him. Monroe, too, had been a soldier and a man of action. Monroe, too, had been frustrated by the Florida problem for some time. He decided that he would stand behind Jackson as much as he could. Secretary of State Adams was given the tough job of explaining things to Britain and Spain. Luckily, Adams was a clever man and a very good talker. He managed to soothe both countries. Another cabinet member wrote a long newspaper article explaining the whole affair to the American people.

Monroe now had to deal with Jackson. He wrote to Jackson that "you acted on your own responsibility." Jackson became huffy. He always felt that he was right. He was very cool to Monroe for a long time afterwards. But because of Monroe's patient and calm manner, he and Jackson were able to remain polite toward each other, although they would never again be friends.

Finally, by 1821, the U.S. owned Florida. Adams had forced Spain to give up the territory, saying that if the Spanish could not keep order there, then America would.

A tobacco plantation in the South

Now a larger problem loomed — the issue of slavery. Before the American Revolution, there had been slaves in all of the thirteen colonies. But slavery did not last in the North. This was partly because people were against it and partly because the land was not suited for the type of farming that required slave labor. Northern farms were smaller than Southern farms, and they usually grew many different crops. Slave labor was suited to large, one-crop farms like those in the South, where large plantations produced all cotton, tobacco, or (in Louisiana) sugarcane.

A slave with his bag of cotton bolls

There had been a time when it looked as though slavery would die out in the South. That had been in the 1790s, when not much cotton was being grown there.

It was hard work to grow cotton. The crop was planted in March. From the time it was planted until the time it was picked, the plants needed constant attention. The cotton bolls, or pods, ripened at different times, so that a field had to be picked two or three times. Slaves crawled up and down the cotton rows on their knees dragging large bags which they filled with cotton bolls. The tough bolls cut the skin easily. And once they were picked, the cotton lint had to be separated from the hard seeds by hand.

Eli Whitney's cotton gin

In 1793, a young man named Eli Whitney invented the cotton gin. ("Gin" was short for "engine.") Whitney's machine separated the cotton seeds from the lint much more quickly than slaves could have done by hand. The gin was fifty times as fast as a man working by hand. Suddenly, raising cotton became very profitable—if slaves were used to plant and harvest it. England was hungry for cotton because Britain had factories with power looms that would weave the cotton into cloth. Now there was no chance that slavery would quietly disappear. The price of slaves for the fields increased sharply. Everyone was planting cotton. Planters were becoming wealthy—thanks to the labor of slaves.

During Monroe's presidency, there were about 1,500,000 slaves in the U.S. The total population was about 9,600,000. The life of a slave was filled with hard work and few pleasures. Slaves could be sold at any time, with or without their families. The law treated them not as persons but as things. They had no say in their future and little hope of freedom unless they succeeded in running away.

Southerners realized that many Northerners hated slavery. They also knew that the Northern states had a larger population than the Southern states. They feared that, one day, Congress would simply vote to wipe out slavery.

Congress has two houses — the House of Representatives and the Senate. The North already had a majority in the House, because the number of representatives a state had there was based on population. In the Senate, it was a different matter. Every state, large and small, could have two senators. The South needed to keep things even in the Senate. They could do this as long as there were as many slave states as free states. There was an unspoken agreement in Congress that the balance must be kept. When a new free state was admitted to the U.S., a new slave state was admitted at the same time. In 1818, there were eleven free states and eleven slave states.

In 1819, trouble began. Missouri asked to come into the U.S. as a slave state. Actually, Missouri did not have the kind of land suited to cotton growing and to slavery. It was better suited for growing grain and vegetables. But the state had been settled by slave-owners and they wished it to be a slave state.

Northerners were bothered by this because they felt that Missouri was in "free soil." Missouri was almost as far north as Indiana, Illinois, and Ohio.

While the bill that would admit Missouri as a state was being discussed in Congress, a Northern representative added something new to the bill. The addition said that no more slaves could be brought into Missouri. It also said that the children of all of the slaves that were already in Missouri would be freed when they became twenty-five years old.

This bill passed in the House, but it failed in the Senate. Missouri was still waiting to become a state. North and South both were becoming angry. A compromise was pieced together. Maine would be admitted as a free state and Missouri would be admitted as a slave state, but slavery would be banned north of the 36′ 30″ latitude. This line was Missouri's southern border. Missouri would be the only Northern slave state, surrounded by free states. The bill squeaked by with a margin of three votes. Would Monroe sign it into law or would he veto it?

Monroe had threatened to veto the bill. In fact, he had already written a veto message. He was, after all, a Southerner who owned slaves. He was also under pressure from his friends, most of whom were Southerners. He had stayed out of the issue while it was being fought in Congress. But now, on March 3, 1820, the bill was before him. He feared that this bill was unconstitutional because it limited the rights of states to decide whether they wished to be free states or slave states. It was Monroe's feeling that "all states, new as well as old, must have equal rights."

He called a cabinet meeting and found no answer. In all of his cabinet, only Adams was really against slavery. Monroe's larger fear was that, if he did not sign the bill, there might be civil war in the country. He wished to avoid this at all costs. So, on March 6, he signed the Missouri Compromise into law, feeling all the while that it was unconstitutional.

In doing so, he lost some friends in the South. He did not even please some Northerners. Secretary of State Adams, who wished all slavery to be ended, thought that the Missouri Compromise was an evil "bargain between freedom and slavery." He called it "morally and politically vicious." Monroe himself saw slavery as wrong. For a while he thought that the answer was to free slaves gradually and take them back to Africa. He supported some societies that believed in this idea. These societies actually bought land in Africa and set it aside for freed slaves. They established the African state of Liberia and named its capital Monrovia after Monroe. At the end of his second term, in 1824, Monroe tried to make slave trade an act of piracy, but this bill did not pass.

Monroe meant well, but none of his efforts to come to grips with slavery succeeded. The campaign to send the slaves back to Africa was a failure. The slaves who actually returned found it very difficult to adjust to Africa. Most of them had never lived in Africa, but were second- or third-generation slaves who had been born in America.

The nation itself struggled on, half slave and half free. Only the Civil War, still forty years away, would provide the solution.

Above: A meeting of the American Colonization Society, organized to return slaves to Africa. Below: A ten-cent Liberian bill

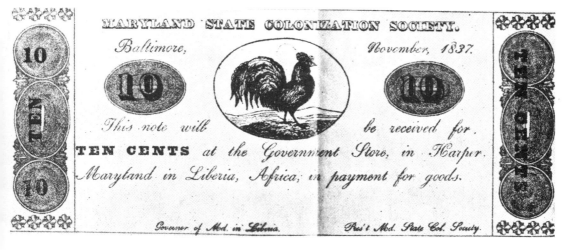

Above: Monrovia, the capital of the Republic of Liberia
Below: A street in Monrovia, around 1885

Chapter 8

The Second Term

March 5, 1821, was a wet, raw, muddy day — too wet for a ceremony outdoors. A huge crowd waited in the House of Representatives. They were there to see James Monroe take the presidential oath for the second time.

No one had run against Monroe; there was no strong opposing party. Monroe saw this as a good sign. He believed that the U.S. had rid itself of the evils of party politics. But he was wrong about this.

Each section of the U.S. was very different from every other section. The West was rural. The East was urban. Westerners and easterners found it hard to agree on anything. North and South were becoming bitterly opposed over slavery. The U.S. had growing pains.

Road building was one issue that split the country. The North and the East had fairly good roads already. Southern and western states needed roads badly, but could not afford to build them. They felt that the federal government should help. Northerners and easterners were reluctant to spend any money building roads in another area of the country.

Roads enabled settlers to open up the West.

The Cumberland Road started in Maryland. Its builders had great plans. But they ran out of money in 1819 and stopped building. The Cumberland stopped in Wheeling, West Virginia. By 1822, the road needed repairs. Henry Clay, who was from Kentucky, introduced a bill into Congress. Clay's bill called for $9,000 for the repairs for the Cumberland Road. But the bill also said that the federal government would build toll booths along the road to collect money for future road repairs.

Congress passed the bill, but to everyone's surprise, President Monroe vetoed it. Westerners felt betrayed and angry. Monroe had always been a champion of western rights. He was still sympathetic to the West, but he felt that this bill was not in line with the U.S. Constitution. Monroe felt sure that collecting road tolls was not a job for the federal government. It was a job for the states.

Monroe's veto started a bitter fight in Congress. Finally, Monroe said that he would not veto the bill if it simply called for road repairs. The bill was changed, so that it no longer said anything about toll booths. When the new bill passed Congress, Monroe signed it.

In 1824, Congress passed a General Survey Bill. The bill set aside $30,000 to be spent planning a system of roads and canals that would be good for the entire nation.

Monroe is not remembered for his successes in domestic policy. He did a good job. He dealt with problems as they arose. But the major problems were not solved during Monroe's presidency. The Missouri Compromise did not settle the issue of slavery. The General Survey Bill did not solve the problem of sectionalism. Wealthy states were still unwilling to help poorer states with road building.

But Monroe did earn a respected place in history for his successes in foreign policy. During his second term, he issued his famous Monroe Doctrine. The doctrine was simple enough. It stated that Americans would not become involved in the wars and politics of foreign countries. But it also stated that the U.S. cared very much about what happened in the Western Hemisphere. Foreign powers were not to meddle with the countries of North or South America. The Monroe Doctrine helped to form American attitudes about how the U.S. and foreign countries should behave toward one another.

A cartoon from the *New York Herald*, captioned "Let it be written so it can be read."

Everyone knew that this was Monroe's last term as president. He did not want a third term. He was proud of his accomplishments and he looked forward to retirement. Monroe's second term should have been a happy time for him. Instead, the second term was made miserable by the constant quarreling of the men who wished to be president after Monroe.

There were five able men who wanted the job. Three of them were in Monroe's cabinet. Monroe hated fighting. During his second term, his own cabinet was the scene of constant bickering and name-calling. His cabinet officers would not help each other with work. Each tried to make the other look bad.

Above: John Quincy Adams, secretary of state

Top right: John C. Calhoun, secretary of war

Right: William Crawford, secretary of the treasury

John Quincy Adams was Monroe's secretary of state. Adams, from New England, was the son of the second president, John Adams. He was brilliant, but he had a cold personality. People did not warm to him. John C. Calhoun was secretary of war. A Southerner, Calhoun stood for Western rights. William Crawford was secretary of the treasury. Crawford was also a Southerner, and a brilliant speaker as well. For a long time, he was the front runner.

Left: Andrew Jackson.   Right: Henry Clay

There were two powerful candidates outside Monroe's cabinet. One was Henry Clay, the Speaker of the House. This Kentuckian had a charming personality, but he had always been unfriendly to James Monroe. It was Clay who had refused to let Monroe take his first oath of office indoors. This was his petty way of trying to ruin Monroe's inauguration ceremony. Now that Clay was running for president, he criticized Monroe more than ever.

Andrew Jackson, the popular hero of the Battle of New Orleans, also pictured himself in the White House. He and Monroe had once been friends. In fact, Monroe had helped him very recently. In 1821, Congress reduced the size of the army in order to save money. Because there were too many generals, Jackson lost his rank as general. Monroe felt badly for him. He stepped in and appointed Jackson the first governor of Florida. Jackson hated life in Florida.

He disliked the weather and he had never liked the Spanish. The Spanish were in the process of leaving Florida, which was now a part of the U.S. The outgoing Spanish governor refused to hand over some papers to Jackson. In his usual hot-headed and arrogant manner, Jackson had the Spanish governor thrown in jail. Monroe was aghast. He was openly critical. But the public wrote angry letters defending Jackson. Jackson finally resigned. He was overjoyed to leave Florida. But after this, he was openly hostile to Monroe.

Monroe was used to the attacks of Henry Clay. He could live with Andrew Jackson's disliking him. But the fighting within his own cabinet was almost unbearable to him. He was careful not to seem to favor any one candidate more than another. He stopped going to parties or dinners that he knew would be attended by one of the candidates, because it might seem that he favored that man.

For a long time, it seemed that William Crawford was sure to win. Then he became ill. A doctor gave him all the old-fashioned treatments of the day and, for a short time, he was both blind and paralyzed. By the time he recovered, he had lost his clear lead.

When the election was held, no one had a majority — that is, over 50 percent of the votes. The House of Representatives had to choose a winner from the top three candidates. These were Jackson, Adams, and Crawford. Clay had come in fourth. He knew he could not win now. But by persuading his supporters to vote for another candidate, he could decide who would win. He threw his votes to Adams. John Quincy Adams would be the next president.

There was a bright spot for James Monroe in the last year of his presidency. The Marquis de Lafayette returned to the U.S. for his first visit since the end of the American Revolution.

Monroe knew that Lafayette could not afford the trip because he had lost his money during the French Revolution. So Monroe asked Congress to help. Congress voted to give Lafayette $200,000 plus some land in Florida. Americans hoped that Lafayette would settle in the U.S. on this land, though he never did.

When Lafayette arrived in New York City, the country went wild. Everywhere he went, parades, large crowds, dinners, and speeches followed. There were souvenir buttons, books, bottles, glasses, medals, and dishes bearing pictures of Lafayette.

On New Year's Day, 1825, Lafayette was the guest of honor at a dinner in Washington. Monroe was the host. He welcomed his old friend warmly, announcing to him, "You will always find your places ready at my table and I wish whenever you have no engagements with citizens that you will dine with me."

Soon after this dinner, John Quincy Adams was sworn in as president. James Monroe left office on March 4, 1825, at the age of sixty-seven.

He left the presidency with no regrets. He was proud of all the things he had done as president, but he was tired of the burdens of public life. He wrote to his friend James Madison, "I shall be heartily rejoiced when the term of my service expires and I may return home in peace with my family."

Above left: The Marquis de Lafayette as
a young soldier in the revolutionary war
Above right: Lafayette in later life
Below: Lafayette visiting Andrew Jackson

The Monroes' Oak Hill estate

Chapter 9

A Final Separation

The Monroes went to live on their family estate near Leesburg, Virginia. Oak Hill, as the estate was named, was thirty-seven miles from the capital. Designed by Thomas Jefferson, the home was a beautiful brick mansion surrounded by hardwood trees and set in rolling hills. On the lawn, there stood an oak tree for every state.

Retirement would have been pleasant, but Monroe had serious money troubles. He was not the only ex-president to have this problem. Jefferson, too, was terribly poor. Public service did not pay well. Monroe had spent a lot of his own money on presidential expenses. He applied to Congress for repayment, but Congress dragged its feet.

Lafayette, now back in France, heard of Monroe's troubles. He wrote to offer him money. But Monroe replied, "My dear friend, I can never take anything from your family."

The Monroes were forced to sell land that they owned in Virginia and Kentucky. Monroe became disgusted with Congress. He no longer even hoped to be repaid.

Monroe's wife, Elizabeth, died on September 23, 1830. Theirs had been a happy marriage, and Monroe never recovered from the loss. The big old house at Oak Hill seemed too big and lonely without Elizabeth. So Monroe moved to New York City to live with his younger daughter, Maria Gouverneur, and her husband. The couple was happy to have him live with them.

Soon, however, Monroe's health declined. He coughed constantly. And he was saddened by the death of his wife and of many of his friends. Thomas Jefferson was dead. He and John Adams had died on the same day — the Fourth of July, 1826.

James Madison was still alive, but Monroe knew that he would never see him again. Both men were too weak to travel. Monroe wrote to Madison: "I deeply regret that there is no prospect of our ever meeting again since so long have we been connected, and in the most friendly intercourse . . . that a final separation is among the most distressing incidents which could occur."

Madison answered: "The pain I feel at the idea [of not meeting Monroe again], associated as it is with a recollection of the long, close, and uninterrupted friendship which united us, amounts to a pang which I cannot well express."

James Monroe died on July 4, 1831. Huge crowds of people attended his funeral in New York City. Bells tolled and gun salutes were fired all over town. Monroe was buried in New York City, but in 1858, just before the Civil War, Virginia asked to have the body moved to his native state. His remains were then moved to a cemetery in Richmond, Virginia.

James Monroe, a man of "many private virtues"

James Monroe never could resist an opportunity to put his talents and his vast energies at the service of his country. In his lifetime he had served the U.S. in many capacities—as a soldier, a diplomat, governor of Virginia, U.S. senator, secretary of state, secretary of war, and president. There have been more brilliant public servants. But in terms of character, James Monroe was second to none. His honesty and sincerity distinguished him.

After Monroe's death, his good friend Madison saluted him. He praised "the comprehensiveness and character of his mind; the purity and nobleness of his principles; the importance of his patriotic services; and the many private virtues of which his whole life was a model."

As another famous friend, Thomas Jefferson, had once observed, Monroe was "so honest that if you turned his soul inside out, there would not be a spot on it."

Chronology of American History

(Shaded area covers events in James Monroe's lifetime.)

About A.D. 982—Eric the Red, born in Norway, reaches Greenland in one of the first European voyages to North America.

About 1000—Leif Ericson (Eric the Red's son) leads what is thought to be the first European expedition to mainland North America; Leif probably lands in Canada.

1492—Christopher Columbus, seeking a sea route from Spain to the Far East, discovers the New World.

1497—John Cabot reaches Canada in the first English voyage to North America.

1513—Ponce de Léon explores Florida in search of the fabled Fountain of Youth.

1519-1521—Hernando Cortés of Spain conquers Mexico.

1534—French explorers led by Jacques Cartier enter the Gulf of St. Lawrence in Canada.

1540—Spanish explorer Francisco Coronado begins exploring the American Southwest, seeking the riches of the mythical Seven Cities of Cibola.

1565—St. Augustine, Florida, the first permanent European town in what is now the United States, is founded by the Spanish.

1607—Jamestown, Virginia, is founded, the first permanent English town in the present-day U.S.

1608—Frenchman Samuel de Champlain founds the village of Quebec, Canada.

1609—Henry Hudson explores the eastern coast of present-day U.S. for the Netherlands; the Dutch then claim parts of New York, New Jersey, Delaware, and Connecticut and name the area New Netherland.

1619—The English colonies' first shipment of black slaves arrives in Jamestown.

1620—English Pilgrims found Massachusetts's first permanent town at Plymouth.

1621—Massachusetts Pilgrims and Indians hold the famous first Thanksgiving feast in colonial America.

1623—Colonization of New Hampshire is begun by the English.

1624—Colonization of present-day New York State is begun by the Dutch at Fort Orange (Albany).

1625—The Dutch start building New Amsterdam (now New York City).

1630—The town of Boston, Massachusetts, is founded by the English Puritans.

1633—Colonization of Connecticut is begun by the English.

1634—Colonization of Maryland is begun by the English.

1636—Harvard, the colonies' first college, is founded in Massachusetts. Rhode Island colonization begins when Englishman Roger Williams founds Providence.

1638—Delaware colonization begins as Swedes build Fort Christina at present-day Wilmington.

1640—Stephen Daye of Cambridge, Massachusetts prints *The Bay Psalm Book*, the first English-language book published in what is now the U.S.

1643—Swedish settlers begin colonizing Pennsylvania.

About 1650—North Carolina is colonized by Virginia settlers.

1660—New Jersey colonization is begun by the Dutch at present-day Jersey City.

1670—South Carolina colonization is begun by the English near Charleston.

1673—Jacques Marquette and Louis Jolliet explore the upper Mississippi River for France.

1682—Philadelphia, Pennsylvania, is settled. La Salle explores Mississippi River all the way to its mouth in Louisiana and claims the whole Mississippi Valley for France.

1693—College of William and Mary is founded in Williamsburg, Virginia.

1700—Colonial population is about 250,000.

1703—Benjamin Franklin is born in Boston.

1732—George Washington, first president of the U.S., is born in Westmoreland County, Virginia.

1733—James Oglethorpe founds Savannah, Georgia; Georgia is established as the thirteenth colony.

1735—John Adams, second president of the U.S., is born in Braintree, Massachusetts.

1737—William Byrd founds Richmond, Virginia.

1738—British troops are sent to Georgia over border dispute with Spain.

1739—Black insurrection takes place in South Carolina.

1740—English Parliament passes act allowing naturalization of immigrants to American colonies after seven-year residence.

1743—Thomas Jefferson is born in Albemarle County, Virginia. Benjamin Franklin retires at age thirty-seven to devote himself to scientific inquiries and public service.

1744—King George's War begins; France joins war effort against England.

1745—During King George's War, France raids settlements in Maine and New York.

1747—Classes begin at Princeton College in New Jersey.

1748—The Treaty of Aix-la-Chapelle concludes King George's War.

1749—Parliament legally recognizes slavery in colonies and the inauguration of the plantation system in the South. George Washington becomes the surveyor for Culpepper County in Virginia.

1750—Thomas Walker passes through and names Cumberland Gap on his way toward Kentucky region. Colonial population is about 1,200,000.

1751—James Madison, fourth president of the U.S., is born in Port Conway, Virginia. English Parliament passes Currency Act, banning New England colonies from issuing paper money. George Washington travels to Barbados.

1752—Pennsylvania Hospital, the first general hospital in the colonies, is founded in Philadelphia. Benjamin Franklin uses a kite in a thunderstorm to demonstrate that lightning is a form of electricity.

1753—George Washington delivers command that the French withdraw from the Ohio River Valley; French disregard the demand. Colonial population is about 1,328,000.

1754—French and Indian War begins (extends to Europe as the Seven Years' War). Washington surrenders at Fort Necessity.

1755—French and Indians ambush Braddock. Washington becomes commander of Virginia troops.

1756—England declares war on France.

1758—James Monroe, fifth president of the U.S., is born in Westmoreland County, Virginia.

1759—Cherokee Indian war begins in southern colonies; hostilities extend to 1761. George Washington marries Martha Dandridge Custis.

1760—George III becomes king of England. Colonial population is about 1,600,000.

1762—England declares war on Spain.

1763—Treaty of Paris concludes the French and Indian War and the Seven Years' War. England gains Canada and most other French lands east of the Mississippi River.

1764—British pass the Sugar Act to gain tax money from the colonists. The issue of taxation without representation is first introduced in Boston. John Adams marries Abigail Smith.

1765—Stamp Act goes into effect in the colonies. Business virtually stops as almost all colonists refuse to use the stamps.

1766—British repeal the Stamp Act.

1767—John Quincy Adams, sixth president of the U.S. and son of second president John Adams, is born in Braintree, Massachusetts. Andrew Jackson, seventh president of the U.S., is born in Waxhaw settlement, South Carolina.

1769—Daniel Boone sights the Kentucky Territory.

1770—In the Boston Massacre, British soldiers kill five colonists and injure six. Townshend Acts are repealed, thus eliminating all duties on imports to the colonies except tea.

1771—Benjamin Franklin begins his autobiography, a work that he will never complete. The North Carolina assembly passes the "Bloody Act," which makes rioters guilty of treason.

1772—Samuel Adams rouses colonists to consider British threats to self-government.

1773—English Parliament passes the Tea Act. Colonists dressed as Mohawk Indians board British tea ships and toss 342 casks of tea into the water in what becomes known as the Boston Tea Party. William Henry Harrison is born in Charles City County, Virginia.

1774—British close the port of Boston to punish the city for the Boston Tea Party. First Continental Congress convenes in Philadelphia.

1775—American Revolution begins with battles of Lexington and Concord, Massachusetts. Second Continental Congress opens in Philadelphia. George Washington becomes commander-in-chief of the Continental army.

1776—Declaration of Independence is adopted on July 4.

1777—Congress adopts the American flag with thirteen stars and thirteen stripes. John Adams is sent to France to negotiate peace treaty.

1778—France declares war against Great Britain and becomes U.S. ally.

1779—British surrender to Americans at Vincennes. Thomas Jefferson is elected governor of Virginia. James Madison is elected to the Continental Congress.

1780—Benedict Arnold, first American traitor, defects to the British.

1781—Articles of Confederation go into effect. Cornwallis surrenders to George Washington at Yorktown, ending the American Revolution.

1782—American commissioners, including John Adams, sign peace treaty with British in Paris. Thomas Jefferson's wife, Martha, dies. Martin Van Buren is born in Kinderhook, New York.

1784—Zachary Taylor is born near Barboursville, Virginia.

1785—Congress adopts the dollar as the unit of currency. John Adams is made minister to Great Britain. Thomas Jefferson is appointed minister to France.

1786—Shays's Rebellion begins in Massachusetts.

1787—Constitutional Convention assembles in Philadelphia, with George Washington presiding; U.S. Constitution is adopted. Delaware, New Jersey, and Pennsylvania become states.

1788—Virginia, South Carolina, New York, Connecticut, New Hampshire, Maryland, and Massachusetts become states. U.S. Constitution is ratified. New York City is declared U.S. capital.

1789—Presidential electors elect George Washington and John Adams as first president and vice-president. Thomas Jefferson is appointed secretary of state. North Carolina becomes a state. French Revolution begins.

1790—Supreme Court meets for the first time. Rhode Island becomes a state. First national census in the U.S. counts 3,929,214 persons. John Tyler is born in Charles City County, Virginia.

1791—Vermont enters the Union. U.S. Bill of Rights, the first ten amendments to the Constitution, goes into effect. District of Columbia is established. James Buchanan is born in Stony Batter, Pennsylvania.

1792—Thomas Paine publishes *The Rights of Man*. Kentucky becomes a state. Two political parties are formed in the U.S., Federalist and Republican. Washington is elected to a second term, with Adams as vice-president.

1793—War between France and Britain begins; U.S. declares neutrality. Eli Whitney invents the cotton gin; cotton production and slave labor increase in the South.

1794—Eleventh Amendment to the Constitution is passed, limiting federal courts' power. "Whiskey Rebellion" in Pennsylvania protests federal whiskey tax. James Madison marries Dolley Payne Todd.

1795—George Washington signs the Jay Treaty with Great Britain. Treaty of San Lorenzo, between U.S. and Spain, settles Florida boundary and gives U.S. right to navigate the Mississippi. James Polk is born near Pineville, North Carolina.

1796—Tennessee enters the Union. Washington gives his Farewell Address, refusing a third presidential term. John Adams is elected president and Thomas Jefferson vice-president.

1797—Adams recommends defense measures against possible war with France. Napoleon Bonaparte and his army march against Austrians in Italy. U.S. population is about 4,900,000.

1798—Washington is named commander-in-chief of the U.S. Army. Department of the Navy is created. Alien and Sedition Acts are passed. Napoleon's troops invade Egypt and Switzerland.

1799—George Washington dies at Mount Vernon, New York. James Monroe is elected governor of Virginia. French Revolution ends. Napoleon becomes ruler of France.

1800—Thomas Jefferson and Aaron Burr tie for president. U.S. capital is moved from Philadelphia to Washington, D.C. The White House is built as presidents' home. Spain returns Louisiana to France. Millard Fillmore is born in Locke, New York.

1801—After thirty-six ballots, House of Representatives elects Thomas Jefferson president, making Burr vice-president. James Madison is named secretary of state.

1802—Congress abolishes excise taxes. U.S. Military Academy is founded at West Point, New York.

1803—Ohio enters the Union. Louisiana Purchase treaty is signed with France, greatly expanding U.S. territory.

1804—Twelfth Amendment to the Constitution rules that president and vice-president be elected separately. Alexander Hamilton is killed by Vice-President Aaron Burr in a duel. Orleans Territory is established. Napoleon crowns himself emperor of France. Franklin Pierce is born in Hillsborough Lower Village, New Hampshire.

1805—Thomas Jefferson begins his second term as president. Lewis and Clark expedition reaches the Pacific Ocean.

1806—Coinage of silver dollars is stopped; resumes in 1836.

1807—Aaron Burr is acquitted in treason trial. Embargo Act closes U.S. ports to trade.

1808—James Madison is elected president. Congress outlaws importing slaves from Africa. Andrew Johnson is born in Raleigh, North Carolina.

1809—Abraham Lincoln is born near Hodgenville, Kentucky.

1810—U.S. population is 7,240,000.

1811—William Henry Harrison defeats Indians at Tippecanoe. Monroe is named secretary of state.

1812—Louisiana becomes a state. U.S. declares war on Britain (War of 1812). James Madison is reelected president. Napoleon invades Russia.

1813—British forces take Fort Niagara and Buffalo, New York.

1814—Francis Scott Key writes "The Star-Spangled Banner." British troops burn much of Washington, D.C., including the White House. Treaty of Ghent ends War of 1812. James Monroe becomes secretary of war.

1815—Napoleon meets his final defeat at Battle of Waterloo.

1816—James Monroe is elected president. Indiana becomes a state.

1817—Mississippi becomes a state. Construction on Erie Canal begins.

1818—Illinois enters the Union. The present thirteen-stripe flag is adopted. Border between U.S. and Canada is agreed upon.

1819—Alabama becomes a state. U.S. purchases Florida from Spain. Thomas Jefferson establishes the University of Virginia.

1820—James Monroe is reelected. In the Missouri Compromise, Maine enters the Union as a free (non-slave) state.

1821—Missouri enters the Union as a slave state. Santa Fe Trail opens the American Southwest. Mexico declares independence from Spain. Napoleon Bonaparte dies.

1822—U.S. recognizes Mexico and Colombia. Liberia in Africa is founded as a home for freed slaves. Ulysses S. Grant is born in Point Pleasant, Ohio. Rutherford B. Hayes is born in Delaware, Ohio.

1823—Monroe Doctrine closes North and South America to European colonizing or invasion.

1824—House of Representatives elects John Quincy Adams president when none of the four candidates wins a majority in national election. Mexico becomes a republic.

1825—Erie Canal is opened. U.S. population is 11,300,000.

1826—Thomas Jefferson and John Adams both die on July 4, the fiftieth anniversary of the Declaration of Independence.

1828—Andrew Jackson is elected president. Tariff of Abominations is passed, cutting imports.

1829—James Madison attends Virginia's constitutional convention. Slavery is abolished in Mexico. Chester A. Arthur is born in Fairfield, Vermont.

1830—Indian Removal Act to resettle Indians west of the Mississippi is approved.

1831—James Monroe dies in New York City. James A. Garfield is born in Orange, Ohio. Cyrus McCormick develops his reaper.

1832—Andrew Jackson, nominated by the new Democratic Party, is reelected president.

1833—Britain abolishes slavery in its colonies. Benjamin Harrison is born in North Bend, Ohio.

1835—Federal government becomes debt-free for the first time.

1836—Martin Van Buren becomes president. Texas wins independence from Mexico. Arkansas joins the Union. James Madison dies at Montpelier, Virginia.

1837—Michigan enters the Union. U.S. population is 15,900,000. Grover Cleveland is born in Caldwell, New Jersey.

1840—William Henry Harrison is elected president.

1841—President Harrison dies in Washington, D.C., one month after inauguration. Vice-President John Tyler succeeds him.

1843—William McKinley is born in Niles, Ohio.

1844—James Knox Polk is elected president. Samuel Morse sends first telegraphic message.

1845—Texas and Florida become states. Potato famine in Ireland causes massive emigration from Ireland to U.S. Andrew Jackson dies near Nashville, Tennessee.

1846—Iowa enters the Union. War with Mexico begins.

1847—U.S. captures Mexico City.

1848—John Quincy Adams dies in Washington, D.C. Zachary Taylor becomes president. Treaty of Guadalupe Hidalgo ends Mexico-U.S. war. Wisconsin becomes a state.

1849—James Polk dies in Nashville, Tennessee.

1850—President Taylor dies in Washington, D.C.; Vice-President Millard Fillmore succeeds him. California enters the Union, breaking tie between slave and free states.

1852—Franklin Pierce is elected president.

1853—Gadsden Purchase transfers Mexican territory to U.S.

1854—"War for Bleeding Kansas" is fought between slave and free states.

1855—Czar Nicholas I of Russia dies, succeeded by Alexander II.

1856—James Buchanan is elected president. In Massacre of Potawatomi Creek, Kansas-slavers are murdered by free-staters. Woodrow Wilson is born in Staunton, Virginia.

1857—William Howard Taft is born in Cincinnati, Ohio.

1858—Minnesota enters the Union. Theodore Roosevelt is born in New York City.

1859—Oregon becomes a state.

1860 — Abraham Lincoln is elected president; South Carolina secedes from the Union in protest.

1861 — Arkansas, Tennessee, North Carolina, and Virginia secede. Kansas enters the Union as a free state. Civil War begins.

1862 — Union forces capture Fort Henry, Roanoke Island, Fort Donelson, Jacksonville, and New Orleans; Union armies are defeated at the battles of Bull Run and Fredericksburg. Martin Van Buren dies in Kinderhook, New York. John Tyler dies near Charles City, Virginia.

1863 — Lincoln issues Emancipation Proclamation: all slaves held in rebelling territories are declared free. West Virginia becomes a state.

1864 — Abraham Lincoln is reelected. Nevada becomes a state.

1865 — Lincoln is assassinated in Washington, D.C., and succeeded by Andrew Johnson. U.S. Civil War ends on May 26. Thirteenth Amendment abolishes slavery. Warren G. Harding is born in Blooming Grove, Ohio.

1867 — Nebraska becomes a state. U.S. buys Alaska from Russia for $7,200,000. Reconstruction Acts are passed.

1868 — President Johnson is impeached for violating Tenure of Office Act, but is acquitted by Senate. Ulysses S. Grant is elected president. Fourteenth Amendment prohibits voting discrimination. James Buchanan dies in Lancaster, Pennsylvania.

1869 — Franklin Pierce dies in Concord, New Hampshire.

1870 — Fifteenth Amendment gives blacks the right to vote.

1872 — Grant is reelected over Horace Greeley. General Amnesty Act pardons ex-Confederates. Calvin Coolidge is born in Plymouth Notch, Vermont.

1874 — Millard Fillmore dies in Buffalo, New York. Herbert Hoover is born in West Branch, Iowa.

1875 — Andrew Johnson dies in Carter's Station, Tennessee.

1876 — Colorado enters the Union. "Custer's last stand": he and his men are massacred by Sioux Indians at Little Big Horn, Montana.

1877 — Rutherford B. Hayes is elected president as all disputed votes are awarded to him.

1880 — James A. Garfield is elected president.

1881 — President Garfield is assassinated and dies in Elberon, New Jersey. Vice-President Chester A. Arthur succeeds him.

1882 — U.S. bans Chinese immigration. Franklin D. Roosevelt is born in Hyde Park, New York.

1884 — Grover Cleveland is elected president. Harry S. Truman is born in Lamar, Missouri.

1885 — Ulysses S. Grant dies in Mount McGregor, New York.

1886 — Statue of Liberty is dedicated. Chester A. Arthur dies in New York City.

1888 — Benjamin Harrison is elected president.

1889 — North Dakota, South Dakota, Washington, and Montana become states.

1890 — Dwight D. Eisenhower is born in Denison, Texas. Idaho and Wyoming become states.

1892 — Grover Cleveland is elected president.

1893 — Rutherford B. Hayes dies in Fremont, Ohio.

1896 — William McKinley is elected president. Utah becomes a state.

1898 — U.S. declares war on Spain over Cuba.

1900 — McKinley is reelected. Boxer Rebellion against foreigners in China begins.

1901 — McKinley is assassinated by anarchist Leon Czolgosz in Buffalo, New York; Theodore Roosevelt becomes president. Benjamin Harrison dies in Indianapolis, Indiana.

1902 — U.S. acquires perpetual control over Panama Canal.

1903 — Alaskan frontier is settled.

1904 — Russian-Japanese War breaks out. Theodore Roosevelt wins presidential election.

1905—Treaty of Portsmouth signed, ending Russian-Japanese War.

1906—U.S. troops occupy Cuba.

1907—President Roosevelt bars all Japanese immigration. Oklahoma enters the Union.

1908—William Howard Taft becomes president. Grover Cleveland dies in Princeton, New Jersey. Lyndon B. Johnson is born near Stonewall, Texas.

1909—NAACP is founded under W.E.B. DuBois

1910—China abolishes slavery.

1911—Chinese Revolution begins. Ronald Reagan is born in Tampico, Illinois.

1912—Woodrow Wilson is elected president. Arizona and New Mexico become states.

1913—Federal income tax is introduced in U.S. through the Sixteenth Amendment. Richard Nixon is born in Yorba Linda, California. Gerald Ford is born in Omaha, Nebraska.

1914—World War I begins.

1915—British liner *Lusitania* is sunk by German submarine.

1916—Wilson is reelected president.

1917—U.S. breaks diplomatic relations with Germany. Czar Nicholas of Russia abdicates as revolution begins. U.S. declares war on Austria-Hungary. John F. Kennedy is born in Brookline, Massachusetts.

1918—Wilson proclaims "Fourteen Points" as war aims. On November 11, armistice is signed between Allies and Germany.

1919—Eighteenth Amendment prohibits sale and manufacture of intoxicating liquors. Wilson presides over first League of Nations; wins Nobel Peace Prize. Theodore Roosevelt dies in Oyster Bay, New York.

1920—Nineteenth Amendment (women's suffrage) is passed. Warren Harding is elected president.

1921—Adolf Hitler's stormtroopers begin to terrorize political opponents.

1922—Irish Free State is established. Soviet states form USSR. Benito Mussolini forms Fascist government in Italy.

1923—President Harding dies in San Francisco, California; he is succeeded by Vice-President Calvin Coolidge.

1924—Coolidge is elected president. Woodrow Wilson dies in Washington, D.C. James Carter is born in Plains, Georgia. George Bush is born in Milton, Massachusetts.

1925—Hitler reorganizes Nazi Party and publishes first volume of *Mein Kampf.*

1926—Fascist youth organizations founded in Germany and Italy. Republic of Lebanon proclaimed.

1927—Stalin becomes Soviet dictator. Economic conference in Geneva attended by fifty-two nations.

1928—Herbert Hoover is elected president. U.S. and many other nations sign Kellogg-Briand pacts to outlaw war.

1929—Stock prices in New York crash on "Black Thursday"; the Great Depression begins.

1930—Bank of U.S. and its many branches close (most significant bank failure of the year). William Howard Taft dies in Washington, D.C.

1931—Emigration from U.S. exceeds immigration for first time as Depression deepens.

1932—Franklin D. Roosevelt wins presidential election in a Democratic landslide.

1933—First concentration camps are erected in Germany. U.S. recognizes USSR and resumes trade. Twenty-First Amendment repeals prohibition. Calvin Coolidge dies in Northampton, Massachusetts.

1934—Severe dust storms hit Plains states. President Roosevelt passes U.S. Social Security Act.

1936—Roosevelt is reelected. Spanish Civil War begins. Hitler and Mussolini form Rome-Berlin Axis.

1937—Roosevelt signs Neutrality Act.

1938—Roosevelt sends appeal to Hitler and Mussolini to settle European problems amicably.

1939—Germany takes over Czechoslovakia and invades Poland, starting World War II.

1940—Roosevelt is reelected for a third term.

1941—Japan bombs Pearl Harbor, U.S. declares war on Japan. Germany and Italy declare war on U.S.; U.S. then declares war on them.

1942—Allies agree not to make separate peace treaties with the enemies. U.S. government transfers more than 100,000 Nisei (Japanese-Americans) from west coast to inland concentration camps.

1943—Allied bombings of Germany begin.

1944—Roosevelt is reelected for a fourth term. Allied forces invade Normandy on D-Day.

1945—President Franklin D. Roosevelt dies in Warm Springs, Georgia; Vice-President Harry S. Truman succeeds him. Mussolini is killed; Hitler commits suicide. Germany surrenders. U.S. drops atomic bomb on Hiroshima; Japan surrenders: end of World War II.

1946—U.N. General Assembly holds its first session in London. Peace conference of twenty-one nations is held in Paris.

1947—Peace treaties are signed in Paris. "Cold War" is in full swing.

1948—U.S. passes Marshall Plan Act, providing $17 billion in aid for Europe. U.S. recognizes new nation of Israel. India and Pakistan become free of British rule. Truman is elected president.

1949—Republic of Eire is proclaimed in Dublin. Russia blocks land route access om Western Germany to Berlin; airlift begins. U.S., France, and Britain agree to merge their zones of occupation in West Germany. Apartheid program begins in South Africa.

1950—Riots in Johannesburg, South Africa, against apartheid. North Korea invades South Korea. U.N. forces land in South Korea and recapture Seoul.

1951—Twenty-Second Amendment limits president to two terms.

1952—Dwight D. Eisenhower resigns as supreme commander in Europe and is elected president.

1953—Stalin dies; struggle for power in Russia follows. Rosenbergs are executed for espionage.

1954—U.S. and Japan sign mutual defense agreement.

1955—Blacks in Montgomery, Alabama, boycott segregated bus lines.

1956—Eisenhower is reelected president. Soviet troops march into Hungary.

1957—U.S. agrees to withdraw ground forces from Japan. Russia launches first satellite, *Sputnik*.

1958—European Common Market comes into being. Fidel Castro begins war against Batista government in Cuba.

1959—Alaska becomes the forty-ninth state. Hawaii becomes fiftieth state. Castro becomes premier of Cuba. De Gaulle is proclaimed president of the Fifth Republic of France.

1960—Historic debates between Senator John F. Kennedy and Vice-President Richard Nixon are televised. Kennedy is elected president. Brezhnev becomes president of USSR.

1961—Berlin Wall is constructed. Kennedy and Khrushchev confer in Vienna. In Bay of Pigs incident, Cubans trained by CIA attempt to overthrow Castro.

1962—U.S. military council is established in South Vietnam.

1963—Riots and beatings by police and whites mark civil rights demonstrations in Birmingham, Alabama; 30,000 troops are called out, Martin Luther King, Jr., is arrested. Freedom marchers descend on Washington, D.C., to demonstrate. President Kennedy is assassinated in Dallas, Texas; Vice-President Lyndon B. Johnson is sworn in as president.

1964—U.S. aircraft bomb North Vietnam. Johnson is elected president. Herbert Hoover dies in New York City.

1965—U.S. combat troops arrive in South Vietnam.

1966—Thousands protest U.S. policy in Vietnam. National Guard quells race riots in Chicago.

1967—Six-Day War between Israel and Arab nations.

1968—Martin Luther King, Jr., is assassinated in Memphis, Tennessee. Senator Robert Kennedy is assassinated in Los Angeles. Riots and police brutality take place at Democratic National Convention in Chicago. Richard Nixon is elected president. Czechoslovakia is invaded by Soviet troops.

1969—Dwight D. Eisenhower dies in Washington, D.C. Hundreds of thousands of people in several U.S. cities demonstrate against Vietnam War.

1970—Four Vietnam War protesters are killed by National Guardsmen at Kent State University in Ohio.

1971—Twenty-Sixth Amendment allows eighteen-year-olds to vote.

1972—Nixon visits Communist China; is reelected president in near-record landslide. Watergate affair begins when five men are arrested in the Watergate hotel complex in Washington, D.C. Nixon announces resignations of aides Haldeman, Ehrlichman, and Dean and Attorney General Kleindienst as a result of Watergate-related charges. Harry S. Truman dies in Kansas City, Missouri.

1973—Vice-President Spiro Agnew resigns; Gerald Ford is named vice-president. Vietnam peace treaty is formally approved after nineteen months of negotiations. Lyndon B. Johnson dies in San Antonio, Texas.

1974—As a result of Watergate cover-up, impeachment is considered; Nixon resigns and Ford becomes president. Ford pardons Nixon and grants limited amnesty to Vietnam War draft evaders and military deserters.

1975—U.S. civilians are evacuated from Saigon, South Vietnam, as Communist forces complete takeover of South Vietnam.

1976—U.S. celebrates its Bicentennial. James Earl Carter becomes president.

1977—Carter pardons most Vietnam draft evaders, numbering some 10,000.

1980—Ronald Reagan is elected president.

1981—President Reagan is shot in the chest in assassination attempt. Sandra Day O'Connor is appointed first woman justice of the Supreme Court.

1983—U.S. troops invade island of Grenada.

1984—Reagan is reelected president. Democratic candidate Walter Mondale's running mate, Geraldine Ferraro, is the first woman selected for vice-president by a major U.S. political party.

1985—Soviet Communist Party secretary Konstantin Chernenko dies; Mikhail Gorbachev succeeds him. U.S. and Soviet officials discuss arms control in Geneva. Reagan and Gorbachev hold summit conference in Geneva. Racial tensions accelerate in South Africa.

1986—Space shuttle *Challenger* explodes shortly after takeoff; crew of seven dies. U.S. bombs bases in Libya. Corazon Aquino defeats Ferdinand Marcos in Philippine presidential election.

1987—Iraqi missile rips the U.S. frigate *Stark* in the Persian Gulf, killing thirty-seven American sailors. Congress holds hearings to investigate sale of U.S. arms to Iran to finance Nicaraguan *contra* movement.

1988—President Reagan and Soviet leader Gorbachev sign INF treaty, eliminating intermediate nuclear forces. Severe drought sweeps the United States. George Bush is elected president.

1989—East Germany opens Berlin Wall, allowing citizens free exit. Communists lose control of governments in Poland, Romania, and Czechoslovakia. Chinese troops massacre over 1,000 pro-democracy student demonstrators in Beijing's Tiananmen Square.

1990—Iraq annexes Kuwait, provoking the threat of war. East and West Germany are reunited. The Cold War between the United States and the Soviet Union comes to a close. Several Soviet republics make moves toward independence.

1991—Backed by a coalition of members of the United Nations, U.S. troops drive Iraqis from Kuwait. Latvia, Lithuania, and Estonia withdraw from the USSR. The Soviet Union dissolves as its republics secede to form a Commonwealth of Independent States.

1992—U.N. forces fail to stop fighting in territories of former Yugoslavia. More than fifty people are killed and more than six hundred buildings burned in rioting in Los Angeles. U.S. unemployment reaches eight-year high. Hurricane Andrew devastates southern Florida and parts of Louisiana. International relief supplies and troops are sent to combat famine and violence in Somalia.

1993—U.S.-led forces use airplanes and missiles to attack military targets in Iraq. William Jefferson Clinton becomes the forty-second U.S. president.

1994—Richard M. Nixon dies in New York City.

Index

Page numbers in boldface type indicate illustrations.

About the Author

Christine Fitz-Gerald has a B.A. in English Literature from Ohio University and a Masters in Management from Northwestern University. She has been employed by the Quaker Oats Co. and by General Mills. Most recently, she was a strategic planner for a division of Honeywell, Inc. in Minneapolis. She now resides in Chicago with her husband and two young children.